Steck-Vaughn
Shutterbug Books
MATH

Which Does Not Belong?

by B. A. Shaver

STECK-VAUGHN
A Harcourt Company

www.steck-vaughn.com

Which one does **not** belong?

Which one does **not** belong?

Which one does **not** belong?

Which one does **not** belong?

Which one does **not** belong?

Which one does **not** belong?

Which one does **not** belong?